CW00457354

arcola
theatre

The Line

by Timberlake Wertenbaker

First performed at Arcola Theatre on 18 November 2009
produced by Arcola Theatre and Karl Sydow

arcola
theatre

Arcola Theatre has been blazing a trail in artistic excellence since its foundation in 2000, and is one of the most respected arts venues in the UK. Arcola has been celebrated for its diverse theatre programme in its ever expanding number of studio spaces. Arcola Theatre holds the unique position of being supported by established theatre literati as well as young innovators and has staged work by actors, writers and directors including Adam Rapp, Ariel Dorfman, Bill Bryden, Bonnie Greer, David Farr, Dominic Dromgoole, Eric Schlosser, Frank McGuinness, Greg Hicks, Helena Kaut-Howson, Jack Shepherd, Kathryn Hunter, Lia Williams, Max Stafford-Clark, Sam Shepard, Sean Holmes, Timberlake Wertenbaker and William Gaskill.

For Arcola Theatre

Artistic Director	Mehmet Ergen
Executive Producer	Leyla Nazli
Executive Director	Ben Todd
Front of House Manager	Gemma Boettger
Youth and Community Projects Manager	Owen Calvert-Lyons
Sustainability Projects Manager	Rachel Carless
Duty Manager	Charlotte Croft
Youth and Community Projects Coordinator	Nicola Hatton
Duty Manager	Laura Hemming Lowe
Marketing and Press Manager	Laura Jukes
Technical Manager	David Salter
General Manager	Catherine Thornborrow
Duty Manager / Box Office Assistant	Harriet Warnock
Venue Technician	Hilary Williamson

With thanks to all our dedicated volunteers and interns

Arcola Theatre is funded by the Arts Council England

Supported by
**ARTS COUNCIL
ENGLAND**

The Line

by Timberlake Wertenbaker

Cast

Selina Cadell	ZOE CLOZIER
Henry Goodman	EDGAR DEGAS
Sarah Smart	SUZANNE VALADON

Creative Team

Director	Matthew Lloyd
Designer	William Dudley
Lighting Designer	Oliver Fenwick
Sound Designer	Steve Mayo
Associate Sound Designer	Gemma Anne Harrison
Costume Supervisor	Margie Bailey
Assistant Costume Supervisor	Annie Pritchard-Gordon
Props Supervisor	Jemma Gardner
Production Manager	Robert Holmes
Stage Manager	Rebekah Kirk
Stage Manager	Tom Wickens
Production Intern	Jessica Stansfield

For their generous assistance on *The Line*, Arcola Theatre would like to thank Chichester Festival Theatre and Marcus Hall Props.

Timberlake Wertenbaker would like to thank
Marina Warner, Sophie Herxheimer, Ed Kemp, Ellen Newman
and all at RADA, Mel Kenyon, Daisy Lewis, Geraldine James,
Clare Lizzimore and Brigid Larmour.

Cast Biographies

Selina Cadell (Zoé Clozier)

Theatre credits include: *The Cherry Orchard* (Brooklyn Academy/Old Vic Theatre); *The Clean House* (Sheffield Crucible Studio); *The Government Inspector* (Chichester Festival Theatre); *The Rivals* (Bristol Old Vic Theatre); *Uncle Vanya/Twelfth Night* (Donmar Warehouse/Brooklyn Academy); *Noises Off* (Comedy Theatre, London); *A Midsummer Night's Dream* (Albery Theatre); *Morning and Evening* (Hampstead Theatre); *New England* (Royal Shakespeare Company); *Stanley, Pericles, The Madness of George III, The Voysey Inheritance, The Cherry Orchard, The Real Inspector Hound/The Critic, The Duchess of Malfi, Othello, Sisterly Feelings, The Life of Galileo* (National Theatre); *Not Quite Jerusalem* (Royal Court Theatre); *Top Girls* (Royal Court Theatre/New York).

Film credits include: *Hereafter, Wild Child, Snowcake, Confetti, Festival, Chromophobia, Matchpoint, Mrs Caldicot's Cabbage War, Mrs Dalloway, The Madness of King George, Prick Up Your Ears, Not Quite Jerusalem.*

Television credits include: *Life of Riley, Doc Martin, Lewis, Midsomer Murders, Spooks* (ITV); *Lab Rats, New Tricks, Thieves Are Us, Catherine Tate Show, The Amazing Mrs Pritchard, The Worst Week of My Life, The Chatterley Affair, Sensitive Skin, Casanova, PD James Murder Room, My Hero, Inspector Linley Mysteries, Down to Earth, People Like Us, As Time Goes By, Great Expectations, Jonathan Creek, Eastenders, Cardiac Arrest, A Bit of Fry and Laurie* (BBC); *Bremner, Bird and Fortune, The Sword of Honour, Rory Bremner Show, The Secret Life of Michael Fry* (Channel 4); *Murphy's Law* (Tiger Aspect); *Foyle's War* (Greenlit Pond); *Rik Mayall Presents: After All* (Granada); *Poirot: The Murder of Roger Ackroyd, Kavanagh QC* (Carlton).

Henry Goodman (Edgar Degas)

Theatre credits include: *Fiddler on the Roof* (Sheffield Crucible and West End); *The Hypochondriac* (Almeida); *The Birthday Party* (Duchess Theatre); *The Producers* (Broadway/Richard Frankel Productions); *Feelgood* (Garrick Theatre and Hampstead Theatre); *Art* (New York and Wyndhams Theatre); *Chicago* (Adelphi Theatre); *Hysteria* (Royal Court Theatre and Duke of York's Theatre); *Fiddler on the Roof* (Sheffield Crucible); *Performances* (Wilton's Music Hall); *Duet for One* (Almeida and West End). For the Royal Shakespeare Company: *Richard III, They Shoot Horses Don't They, Everyman in his Humour, Henry, The Devils, Redstar, Comedy of Errors, Volpone, The Time of Your Life, Jacques and His Master,* and *Henry VIII.* For the National Theatre: *The Merchant of Venice, Metropolitan Kabarett, Summerfolk, Guys and Dolls, Broken Glass, Angels in America, Pericles, After the Fall, Cat on a Hot Tin Roof, Beatrice and Benedick.*

Television credits include: *Mayor of Casterbridge, Foyle's War, The Merchant of Venice, Secret Weapon, Hamilton Mattress, Murder Rooms, Dalziel and Pascoe, Dirty Tricks, The Arabian Nights, Unfinished Business, Cold Lazarus, Broken Glass, Measure for Measure, Degas and Pissarro Fall Out, 99-1, Lovejoy, Spinoza, Maigret, The Gravy Train II, Gentlemen and Players, London's Burning, This is David Lander, Bust, After the War, The Chain, Keen Eddie,* and most recently *Something for Nothing: The Fall of Lehman Brothers.*

Film credits include: *Colour Me Kubrick, Out on a Limb, The Final Curtain, The Labyrinth, Notting Hill, Private Parts, The Saint, Mary Reilly, Queen of Hearts, Son of Pink Panther, Damned United* and *Taking Woodstock*.

Radio credits: Henry is a leading contributor to BBC Radio Arts, Drama and Readings including the recent *The Shape of the Table* and the Le Carré spy series.

Sarah Smart (Suzanne Valadon)

Theatre credits include: *Ghosts*.

Film and television credits include: *Identity, Casualty 1909, Miss Marple, Wallander, Poirot, City of Vice, Billy Goats Gruff, Whistleblowers, Yellow House, Five Days, Funland, Murder Prevention, Jane Hall, Love Again, Sparkhouse, At Home with the Braithwaites, David Copperfield, Wuthering Heights, Deadly Summer, Ball Trap on the Cote Sauvage, Safe House, Sweet Revenge, Dalziel & Pascoe, The Bill, Soldier, Soldier VII, Bliss, The Locksmith, A Touch of Frost, Chase the Fade, Woof*.

Radio credits include: *Blood Wedding, Safety Catch, Martha's Metamorphosis, Madame Bovary, Strike, Miscreant Mothers, The Living and the Dead, The Provoked Wife, Another Big Day, The Beehive, 'Shubbery Skullduggery.'*

Creative Team Biographies

Timberlake Wertenbaker (Playwright)

Timberlake grew up in the Basque country near Saint-Jean-de-Luz.

Theatre credits include: *The Third* (Kings Head Theatre); *Case to Answer* (Soho Poly Theatre); *New Anatomies* (The Women's Theatre Group, Institute of Contemporary Arts); *Abel's Sister* [Thames TV Award], *The Grace of Mary, Traverse* [Plays & Players Most Promising Playwright Award], *Three Birds Alighting on a Field* [Susan Smith Blackburn, Writers' Guild, and London Critics' Circle Awards], *Credible Witness* (Royal Court Theatre); *Our Country's Good* (Royal Court Theatre/Garrick Theatre [Olivier Play of the Year Award] / Broadway [New York Drama Critics' Circle Award for Best Foreign Play] / tour); *The Break of Day* (Out of Joint/Royal Court Theatre/tour); *The Love of the Nightingale* [Eileen Anderson Central TV Award 1989] (Royal Shakespeare Company); *After Darwin* (Hampstead Theatre); *Ash Girl* (Birmingham Repertory Theatre); *Galileo's Daughter* (Theatre Royal, Bath); *Jenufa* (Arcola); *Mephisto* [Mnouchkine, translation] (Royal Shakespeare Company); *Oedipus Tyrannos, Oedipus at Kolonos, Antigone* [Sophocles, translation] (Royal Shakespeare Company); *Hecuba* [Euripides, Adaptation] (American Conservatory Theatre, San Francisco); *Filumena* [de Philippo, translation] (Piccadilly Theatre); *Wild Orchids* [Anouilh, translation] (Chichester Festival Theatre); *Phèdre* [Racine, Translation] (Stratford Festival, Ontario).

Film credits include: *The Children* [Edith Wharton, adaptation]; *Do Not Disturb* [original screenplay, BBC].

Radio credits include: *New Anatomies* [based on stage play], *La Dispute* [Marivaux, translation], *Pelleas and Melisande* [Maeterlinck, translation], *Madame Paradis* [short story], *Dianeira* (Catherine Bailey Production for the BBC), *The File on H* [Kadare, adaptation], *Scenes of Seduction*.

Opera credits include: *The Love of the Nightingale, The Libretto* (Perth festival).

Matthew Lloyd (Director)

Matthew is Artistic Director of the Actors Centre and one of the UK's leading freelance directors. He was previously Artistic Director of the Royal Exchange Theatre, Manchester, during which time the venue was awarded Theatre of the Year, and Associate Director of Hampstead Theatre.

Theatre credits include: *Duet for One* (Almeida Theatre/national tour/West End transfer to Vaudeville Theatre); *Hedda Gabler, Dead Funny, A Doll's House* (West Yorkshire Playhouse); *The Odd Couple, Fly* (Liverpool Everyman Theatre); *The Dispute and the Critic, The Way of the World, Two Clouds Over Eden, Waiting for Godot, Dreaming, So Special, An Experiment with An Airpump, Present Laughter, The Illusion* [Tony Kushner adaptation], *All's Well That Ends Well, An Experienced Woman Gives Advice* (Royal Exchange Theatre, Manchester); *Vincent River, An Experiment with an Airpump* [London transfer], *Apocalyptica, The Eleventh Commandment, The Maiden Stone, Slavs!, Ghost from a Perfect Place, A Going Concern, Lion in the Streets, The Fastest Clock in the Universe* (Hampstead Theatre); *The Pitchfork Disney* (Bush Theatre); *The LA Plays* (Almeida Theatre); *2 Samuel II* (Theatre Upstairs); *The Home Show Pieces, La Ronde* (Citizens Theatre); *Cloud 9* (Parco Theatre, Tokyo); *A Midsummer Night's Dream* (Haymarket Theatre, Leicester); *Democracy* (Gate Theatre); *Deathwatch* [by Jean Genet], and *Measure for Measure* (Off-Broadway).

Opera credits include: *The Barber of Seville* (Scottish Opera Go Round).

William Dudley (Designer)

Theatre credits include: Over sixty productions for the National Theatre, including six Olivier Awards and a Critics' Circle Award; eighteen productions for London's West End, including an Olivier Award and a Theatregoers' Choice Award for Best Set Designer; twelve productions for the Royal Court Theatre, including a Drama Award; and ten productions for the Royal Shakespeare Company, including an Olivier Award. Other theatre credits include *Look Back In Anger* (Theatre Royal, Bath); *Marya* (Old Vic Theatre); *Amadeus* (Old Vic Theatre/Los Angeles/New York); *The Deep Blue Sea, Tongue Of A Bird* (Almeida Theatre); *Titus Andronicus* (Globe Theatre); *Some Sunny Day, The Giant* (Hampstead Theatre); *The Ship* [for Cultural Capital of Europe Year 1990: Theatre Crafts International Award] (Glasgow); *The Big Picnic* [Harland and Wolff Shipyard 1994] (Glasgow); *Hamlet* (Neues Schauspielhaus Hamburg); and *The Dance Of The Vampires* [Roman Polanski's musical version] (Vienna 1997/Germany tour 2006).

Opera credits include: *Tales of Hoffman, Der Rosenkavalier, Don Giovanni, The Cunning Little Vixen* (Royal Opera House); *The Silver Tassie* (English National Opera); *The Seraglio, The Barber of Seville* (Glyndebourne); *The Barber of Seville, Idomeneo, The Flying Dutchman, Anna Christie* (Welsh National Opera); *Billy Budd* (Metropolitan Opera); *Lucia di Lammermoor* (Lyric Opera of Chicago);

The Ring Cycle (Bayreuth); *Un Ballo in Maschera* (Salzburg Festival); and *Lucia di Lammermoor* (Opera National de Paris).

Film credits include: *Persuasion* [Bafta Award & Royal Television Society Award] (BBC Television & US Cinema, 1994); *The History of the 1587 Rose Theatre* (1999); and *Scenes from Marlowe's Plays at The Rose Theatre* (2008).

Oliver Fenwick (Lighting Designer)

Theatre credits include: *Julius Caesar, The Drunks, The Grain Store* (Royal Shakespeare Company); *The Contingency Plan* (Bush Theatre); *Hedda Gabler* (Gate Theatre, Dublin); *Happy Now?* (National Theatre); *Private Lives, The Giant, Glass Eels, Comfort Me With Apples* (Hampstead Theatre); *Endgame* (Everyman Liverpool Theatre); *Far From The Madding Crowd* (English Touring Theatre); *Lady From The Sea, She Stoops To Conquer* (Birmingham Repertory Theatre); *The Elephant Man* (Lyceum Theatre, Sheffield/tour); *Kean* (Apollo Theatre); *Pure Gold* (Soho Theatre); *Henry V, Mirandolina, A Conversation* (Royal Exchange Theatre); *Restoration* (Bristol Old Vic Theatre/Headlong tour); The Caretaker (*Tricycle Theatre*); *Comedy of Errors, Bird Calls, Iphigenia* (Crucible Theatre, Sheffield); *The Doll's House* (West Yorkshire Playhouse); *Sunshine on Leith* (Dundee Repertory Theatre/tour); *Heartbreak House* (Watford Palace Theatre); *The Solid Gold Cadillac* (Garrick Theatre); *The Secret Rapture* (Lyric Theatre, Shaftesbury Avenue); *Noises Off, All My Sons, Dr. Faustus* (Liverpool Playhouse); *The Chairs* (Gate Theatre); *Follies, Insignificance, Breaking the Code* (Theatre Royal, Northampton); *Tartuffe, The Gentleman From Olmedo, The Venetian Twins, Hobson's Choice, Dancing at Lughnasa,* and *Love in a Maze* (Watermill Theatre, Newbury).

Opera credits include: *Samson et Delilah, Lohengrin* (Royal Opera House); *The Trojan Trilogy, The Nose* (Royal Opera House, Linbury Studio); *The Gentle Giant* (Royal Opera House, Clore Studio).

Steve Mayo (Sound Designer)

Theatre credits include: *Fight Face* (Decibel Festival); *Teenager of the Year* (Latitude Festival 2009); *Guardians, The Fixer, Muhmah* (High Tide Festival 2009); *Miniaturists, Silence* (Arcola Theatre); *Lie of the Land* (Arcola/Edinburgh Festival Fringe2008); *Stovepipe* (W12 Centre, Shepherds Bush/High Tide Festival 2008); *Well* (Apollo Theatre); *I Caught Crabs in Walberswick* (Bush Theatre/High Tide Festival 2008/Edinburgh Festival Fringe 2008); *Public Property; Ordinary Dreams; Sh*t M*x, Snowbound* (Trafalgar Studios); *Fight Face* (Lyric Studio); *Lough/Rain* (Edinburgh Festival 2008); *Hangover Square, Eden's Empire* (Finborough Theatre); *Absolutely Frank* (Queen's Theatre, Hornchurch); *Jack and the Beanstalk* (Barbican Theatre); *Romeo and Juliet* (Battersea Arts Centre); *Future/Perfect* (Soho Theatre); *Weightless, You Were After Poetry, Lyre* and *Ned & Sharon* (High Tide Festival 2007); *Mythomania* (White Bear Theatre); *A Tale of Two Cities, Cinderella* (Guildhall School of Music and Drama); *Dr Foster* (Menier Chocolate Factory); *Stars in the Morning Sky, Three Birds Alighting on a Field* (Mountview Academy of Theatre Arts); *Small Change* (Haymarket Theatre, Basingstoke); *Sleeping Beauty, Taking Sides, Communicating Doors* (Library Theatre, Manchester) and *Rocking Robin* (Liverpool Everyman Theatre).

Composition credits include: *Guardians, Fixer* (High Tide Festival 2009); *Lie of The Land* (Arcola); *Simpatico* (Old Red Lion Theatre); and *Absolutely Frank* (Queen's Theatre).

Gemma Anne Harrison (Associate Sound Designer)

Gemma recently graduated from the Guildhall School of Music and Drama, London, where she specialised in theatre lighting design and sound design and operation for a BA in Stage Management and Technical Theatre. Gemma is also a dedicated musician and was tutored by jazz pianist John Law and classical concert pianist Catalina Ardelean.

Theatre credits include: *Six of One* (lighting, sound, and audio visual design/ operation, King's Head Theatre); *Write Side Of The Brain Festival* (lighting design/operation, Baron's Court Theatre); *Arrows* (lighting and sound design/ operation, Greenwich Playhouse); *Two* (lighting and sound design/operation, Pentameters Theatre, Hampstead); *Lord of the Flies* [sound design], *The Man Who* [sound design], *Hard Times* [lighting design] (Bridewell Theatre, London.); *Damn Yankees* (head of sound/sound number 1, Guildhall School of Music and Drama); *Stovepipe* (sound assistant, Bush Theatre); *Ordinary Dreams* (sound associate, Trafalgar Studios); *Fight Face* (sound associate, Young Actors Theatre, London/LibraryTheatre, Manchester).

Margie Bailey (Costume Supervisor)

Theatre credits include: *Wicked* (London, Germany, Australia); *Peter Pan* (Kensington Gardens and O2); *Spring Awakening* (Lyric Hammersmith and Novello Theatre).

Annie Pritchard-Gordon (Assistant Costume Supervisor)

Annie graduated from Central Saint Martins in 2008.

Theatre credits include: *Wicked* (Apollo Victoria Theatre).

TV credits include: *Tale of Two Cities* (In Concert).

Jemma Gardner (Props Supervisor)

Jemma is a freelance Prop Supervisor, Buyer & Maker. After leaving her job at Thames Water as a civil engineer to train at RADA in Stage Management & Technical Theatre, she worked as a Stage Manager and in various production roles as well as an Event Co-ordinator for the World Scout Jamboree.

Props credits include: *Separate Tables, Grapes of Wrath, Hayfever, House of Special Purpose, Wallenstein, Collaboration, Taking Sides, Calendar Girls, The Circle, Cherry Orchard, Aristo, 6 Characters in Search of An Author* (Props Supervisor, Chichester Festival Theatre); *La Bohème, Iolanthe, Le Roi* and *Malgré Lui* (Props Supervisor, Grange Park Opera); *Harvest* (Prop Buyer, tour); ShowWorks construction co, Melbourne (Prop Maker); Chichester Festival Theatre (Prop Maker, two seasons).

Stage Manager credits include: *House of Agnes* (Paines Plough Theatre Company); *Fingerprint* (Shout Choir UK tour); *Blasted* (UK tour); *Billy Liar* (Liverpool Playhouse); *Only Available in Carlisle* (Theatre by the Lake tour); *Fewer Emergencies* (Royal Court Theatre); *The Death of Gogol and the 1969 Eurovision Song Contest* (Drill Hall); *Il Ritorno d'Ulisse in Patria* (Snape Maltings, Suffolk/Shakespeare's Globe

Theatre); *The Butcher's Skin* (Yellow Earth Theatre, London); *Tall Stories* (Shout Choir international tour); *Votzek* (Birmingham Opera Company); Revelations (Tara Arts UK tour).

Other credits include: *Enron, Oklahoma, Cyrano de Bergerac, Music Man, Funny Girl* (Workshop Manager, Chichester Festival Theatre); *Hamlet* (Production Assistant, National Theatre).

Robert Holmes (Production Manager)

Theatre credits include: Resident Production Manager at the Bush Theatre, managing 26 new plays between 2005 and 2008 including *Elling, Pumpgirl, Crooked, Bottle Universe* and *Kingfisher Blue*. Other theatre credits include *Timing* (Kings Head Theatre); *House of Agnes, Shoot/Get Treasure/Repeat, After The End* (Paines Plough Theatre Company); *Whipping It Up* (New Ambassadors Theatre/tour); *Moby Dick* (Spymonkeys tour); *East, Divine* (Haymarket Theatre, Leicester); *Peter Pan, Cinderella* (Qdos at His Majesty's Theatre, Aberdeen).

Opera credits include: *The Enchanted Pig* (in preparation, New Victory Theater, New York); *The Lions Face* (in preparation, Opera Group tour); *Into The Little Hill, Down by the Greenwood side* (Opera Group and ROH II at the Royal Opera House); *Carmen, The Marriage of Figaro, La Bohéme, La Traviata, The Coronation of Poppea, Das Rheingold* (Longborough Festival Opera); *A Midsummer Night's Dream* and *The Cunning Little Vixen* (Opera Project).

Film credits include: *Finding Neverland* (flying cast on set); *One Day* (short festival film 2007, Logistics Manager).

Rebekah Kirk (Stage Manager)

Theatre credits include: *The Shawl, Ghosts or Those Who Return* (Arcola Theatre); *Fanny and Faggot* (Finborough Theatre/Trafalgar Studios); *Stacy, Some Kind of Bliss, Angry Young Man* (Trafalgar Studios); *Tinderbox, Broken Space Season* (Bush Theatre); *Sleeping Beauty* (The Theatre, Chipping Norton); *Tri-ANGLE New Writers Season* (Hackney Empire Studio); *It's a Girl* (Bucharest International Theatre Festival); *The Lion Hunt, Sing! 2006* (London Coliseum); *John and Jen* (Finborough Theatre); *An Age of Angels* (Assembly Rooms, Edinburgh); *Look Back In Anger* (Jermyn Street Theatre); *Pass The Baton* (Theatre Royal, Stratford East); *They Shoot Horses, Don't They?* (George Wood Theatre); *Big Maggie* (Pentameters Theatre/Ireland tour); *Can't Pay? Won't Pay!, Teechers, Hound of the Baskervilles, Great Expectations* (Brockley Jack Theatre); *Relative Values* and *Dinner* (Brockley Jack Theatre/Greenwich Playhouse).

Tom Wickens (Stage Manager)

Tom Wickens trained at the Academy of Live and Recorded Arts (ALRA) and works as a lighting designer, technician and stage manager in London.

Theatre credits include: *Ghosts, The Shawl, It Felt Empty* (Arcola Theatre); *Paco Peña – Flamenco Sin Fronteras* (Sadler's Wells Theatre); *Ellen Terry; The Children's Opera* (St Paul's Church Covent Garden); *The Scandalous Case of Dr Jekyll & Mr Hyde* (St Augustine's, Edinburgh). Credits at ALRA include *After Mrs Rochester; Daisy Pulls It Off; Unprotected* (Lighting Designer).

Jessica Stansfield (Production Intern, Arcola)

Jessica Stansfield is in her final year at Boston University and currently studying as part of the Boston University London Program.

Theatre credits include: *Military 4Play, Once on this Island, Busytown* (Hangar Theatre, New York); *The New Century, Blackbird* (SpeakEasy Stage Company, Boston); and the world premiere of *The Wrestling Patient* (co-produced with SpeakEasy Stage Company, Boston Playwrights Theatre and Forty Magnolias Productions).

Karl Sydow (Co-Producer)

Theatre credits include: *The Seagull, All My Sons, American Buffalo, Our Country's Good* [six Tony nominations, New York Critics' Award for Best Foreign Play, Olivier Award for Best Play] (Broadway); *Terra Haute* (Off Broadway); *Happy Days* [National Theatre production] (Brooklyn Academy of Music); *Memory, Triptych, Ring Round the Moon* (Playhouse Theatre); *Jenufa* (Arcola). Other theatre credits include: *Dirty Dancing, Sinatra* (London Palladium); *And Then There Were None, Dance of Death* (London and Sydney); *Bea Arthur* (Savoy Theatre); *Auntie and Me, Michael Moore Live!* (Roundhouse); *Semi Monde* (West End premiere); *Mouth to Mouth; Speed the Plow; Drummers, Some Explicit Polaroids, Macbeth, A Swell Party* [celebration of Cole Porter] (Vaudeville Theatre); *Hysteria* [Best Comedy, Olivier Awards]; *The Queen and I.*

Film credits include: *A Bunch of Amateurs* [co-produced with David Parfitt and Trademark Films].

Karl serves on the board of Out of Joint, the UK's leading producer of new writing for the theatre.

Timberlake Wertenbaker
The Line

ff

faber and faber

First published in 2009
by Faber and Faber Limited
74–77 Great Russell Street
London WC1B 3DA

Typeset by Country Setting, Kingsdown, Kent CT14 8ES
Printed in England by CPI Bookmarque, Croydon, Surrey

A CIP record for this book
is available from the British Library

ISBN 978-0-571-25913-7

2 4 6 8 10 9 7 5 3 1

For Henry Goodman,
without whom . . .

Characters

Zoé Clozier
Suzanne Valadon
Edgar Degas

Paris, 1888–1917

THE LINE

This edition of the play text went to press
before the end of rehearsals, so may differ slightly
from the play as performed.

SCENE ONE

'*Young Woman with an Envelope*'

1888. Zoé in black, formidable and immovable.
Suzanne Valadon in slightly garish clothes with an
extravagant hat. She holds a large envelope.

Zoé No. No and no.

Suzanne does not move.

He will not see anyone today.
He won't see anyone tomorrow either. He has a cold.

Suzanne I need to see him.

Zoé He doesn't need to see you.

Suzanne I have something for him.

Zoé He has everything he needs.

Suzanne And I have a letter, it's from a friend of his.

Zoé Everyone has a letter from a friend. Everyone wants
a piece of him, especially the ladies. They rustle their skirts
at him but he has to keep working. He doesn't want to
see a lot of ladies and he never sees a lady in the morning.

Suzanne I'm no lady, you might have noticed that. (*She
laughs.*) I'm definitely not a lady.

Zoé You're wearing a lady's hat.

Suzanne Oh that. Lautrec makes me wear it.

She takes her hat off and shakes out some rather
beautiful hair. Zoé plants herself even more firmly.

9

Zoé He has all the models he needs.

Suzanne I'm not here to model.

Zoé I think I've seen you standing in the Place Pigalle, but he never picks up models from the Place Pigalle, he says they look too eager.

Suzanne Well, they're hungry, aren't they?

Pause.

I won't leave the house until I've given him – this.

Zoé You can leave it with me.

Suzanne I can't leave this with you. I'll wait.

Zoé This is an artist's house.

Suzanne That's why I'll wait.
I can stand still for hours and I'm very strong, so you can't push me out. And he won't like it if you call the police so you better tell him I'm here.

Zoé I'm used to dealing with people who come to bother him. I've been doing it for years. We get beggars, we get whores, we get dealers, we get Americans, all the riff-raff of Montmartre try to disturb Monsieur Degas. But I'm here. Go!

Suzanne No.

Zoé How dare you behave like this?

Suzanne Oh, this is nothing.

Zoé Get out!

Suzanne I'm staying here.

Suzanne doesn't move. Degas comes on, watches for a moment. They see him.

Zoé (*to Suzanne*) Look at what you've done. Aren't you ashamed of yourself? (*To Degas.*) This girl is refusing to leave, but don't worry, I'll deal with her. You can go back upstairs.

Degas Hasn't anyone taught you never to bother a man with a cold? It's getting worse, Zoé.

Zoé I'll bring you a tisane.
Can't you see Monsieur Degas isn't feeling well?

Degas studies Suzanne from a short-sighted closeness. Suzanne remains very still.

Degas Who are you?

Zoé She's a model from the Place Pigalle.

Suzanne Monsieur Bartholomé sent me.

Degas Bartholomé? I haven't seen him in ages. I neglected him when his wife was dying. I don't have a very good heart, Mademoiselle, it gets rusty because I never polish it. I heard he was making some beautiful sculptures, are you modelling for him?

Suzanne He wants you to see – this.

Degas Why didn't he come himself?

Suzanne Henri de Toulouse-Lautrec also told me to come.

Degas That name is not a recommendation. I'm not interested in cartoons.

Suzanne He worships you. The other night he knelt before one of your paintings. He was very drunk but he made us all kneel.

Degas Zoé, my chest is hurting. I think I have bronchitis.

Suzanne And then Monsieur Zandomeneghi also –

Degas Poor Zandomeneghi, trying so hard to paint something real, but he's a Venetian and his bidets always look like flower pots. You seem to have a lot of friends, Mademoiselle.

Suzanne They want me to show you these – these drawings.

Degas Whose drawings? Bartholomé's, Lautrec's? I'm confused. I have a headache.

Zoé I told her to leave the envelope with me.

Suzanne Mine . . . they're my drawings.

Zoé Monsieur Degas already spends too much time with ladies who paint. They're very demanding, especially the rich American ones. But at least they're ladies.

Suzanne Bartholomé told me to insist.

Degas My eyes are bad. You cannot know what a torment it is. When I hear them play music by that depressing Herr van Beethoven, I can tell he was deaf. Is that what they'll say about my work? That I was going blind?

Zoé You know very well they won't say any such thing as long as you're left in peace and you're not made to look at anything you don't want to.

Degas The ache throbs there, behind my eyes. It's very painful. Perhaps another time?

Zoé Quite: Monsieur Degas will see you another time. That ought to be enough.

Suzanne If you look at one drawing, I'll go immediately.

Degas You're very determined.

He takes the envelope and goes to the light.

Suzanne I've had to be. I became an acrobat in the circus when I was fifteen. That takes determination.

Degas Determination is a virtue but it's dangerous.

Suzanne I know. I fell. I was on my back for six months and I couldn't be an acrobat any more so I became a model.

Zoé I told you he doesn't want a model.

Degas takes out a drawing and glances at it. He looks more closely. He takes out the drawings one by one and studies them. Pause. Suzanne now begins to fidget.

Suzanne If your eyes are hurting, I will come back another time.

Degas Silence.

He looks closely at a drawing.

Zoé, you may leave us.

Zoé Are you sure? (*To Suzanne.*) Don't tire him.

She leaves, a slight flounce. Degas looks at the drawing.

Degas What school did you attend?

Suzanne The convent in the Rue Caulaincourt. I found the graveyard opposite was more lively so I got kicked out when I was fourteen.

Degas I mean, where did you learn to draw?

Suzanne I always drew.

Degas Answer me properly. Who taught you?

Suzanne I lived with Puvis de Chavannes and I watched him work. And I posed for Renoir before he married that stupid fat girl. I used to watch him. And when I was a child, I watched all the painters in Montmartre.

Degas This nude is very ugly.

Suzanne I draw what I see.

Pause.

I'll go now.

Degas Does your mother draw?

Suzanne My mother cleans houses.

Degas Your father?

Suzanne I never had a father.
You know those books that teach you to draw? I found some in one of the studios my mother cleaned and I borrowed them – well, I stole them.

Degas 'How to' books . . . All the artists I have ever known are well educated, including the women. Mary Cassatt went to the best fine arts institute in America – Berthe Morisot studied with Corot. Look at Puvis, Pissarro, Manet – we spent our youth in a studio, learning, practising, acquiring the skill to draw a line, being criticised, starting again. And then years studying the Old Masters in the Louvre, endlessly copying their paintings. You spent those years in a circus.

Suzanne It was a very good circus and the horses taught me a lot and they were very kind and – well – I came, didn't I? And now they can all stop pestering me and I won't bother you any more –

Degas How then did you learn to draw a line that is so ferocious and so supple?

Pause.

There is no question, no question at all, Mademoiselle.
You are one of us.

Suzanne You mean –?
You mean –

Degas What I said. You are one of us.

Suzanne suddenly dances around and kisses his hand.

Suzanne Thank you! Thank you. I thought – you looked so stern – I didn't want to say it but I am serious. I've always drawn. I could never stop, even as a child, with chalk on the streets, on walls, scraps of paper. I have to do it but I never dared believe – I've never taken myself seriously because – I mean I did, but I didn't –

Degas You must take yourself very seriously from now on. What is your name?

Suzanne Suzanne Valadon. It's really Marie but I became Maria because that's a better name for a model, but Suzanne sounds more serious.

Degas Suzanne is a very serious name, although I also like Maria.

Suzanne But Suzanne is a good name for an artist, isn't it? I can call myself Suzanne now, now that I'm . . . now that you . . . now?

Degas You can draw, Suzanne, but can you work?
I want to see more drawings next week.

Suzanne You want me to come back next week?

Degas I want more drawings to come back. And would you leave this one with me? I might buy it.

Suzanne You can have it. You can have anything you want from me.

Degas We give drawings to our friends but I'm not your friend. I will buy it. Zoé will see you out. Work.

He hands the envelope back to Suzanne and leaves.

Work . . .

Suzanne is alone for a moment with the envelope. Zoé in the shadows, watching her.

SCENE TWO

'Model and Artist'

Some months later. Degas' studio. A mess. Chairs, a tub. A screen. Drawings and paintings.

Degas and Suzanne. He is showing her a drawing: after the bath, woman drying herself.

Degas She complains it's freezing in here and that she catches colds. She hasn't come for a week. I can't continue without Pauline.

It's the back. Women's backs are strange. They're not feminine but they're not masculine either. Look: the back is wrong here. You can always get out of trouble with colour but the line, the line is always difficult. And I don't know where to place the arm. I could ask someone else but she's the best, she can hold still for hours even if she moans all the time. I don't know what to do, my eyes get worse by the day, I have a cough, how dare she have a cold?

A doorbell rings. He shows Suzanne another drawing.

This one's almost good. I managed to get the hair right. What am I going to do without Pauline, without Pauline's back?

Doorbell more insistent.

Zoé's out. I told her to go find Pauline and drag her here.

Doorbell.

What's the point of cultivating a reputation for rudeness if it doesn't keep people away? It's probably a journalist

16

who thinks I want to be famous. I don't want to be famous, I want to be renowned but unknown.

But a good bourgeois must always open the door – if only to bark.

Wait here.

He goes out. Suzanne studies the unfinished drawing. She traces over it in the air. Then she takes on bits of the pose, bending her back, raising her arm, etc. Suddenly, she goes behind the screen, undresses quickly, comes back out wrapped in a towel and takes the exact pose, a view from the back. It is quite contorted and difficult. She stays very still.

Degas comes back, talking as he enters.

Degas They want me to show a painting at the Universal Exposition but I said no. I refuse to compete with the Eiffel Tower. I was thinking you seem to understand women's backs from the inside but you're still too abrupt, you see, the curve –

He sees and stops.

Suzanne It's a very difficult pose to hold, Monsieur Degas, but I can do it. I can hold poses for hours. I don't think my back is that different. It will help you get the contours anyway.

Degas looks at the drawing and at Suzanne.

Degas How did you get the pose so exactly? It takes me hours to place Pauline.

Suzanne I could see from the drawing. But you have to place the arm.

She holds out her arm.

Degas Yes, the arm.

He displaces one of the arms, moving it around the body.

17

Suzanne Or here . . .

She places it and Degas moves his hand along the arm.

Degas I can draw this arm, I can see its line.
The curve of beauty.

Suzanne looks up to him, open. A moment.

Get dressed!

Suzanne I only moved my head, I didn't move my body.

Degas I said get dressed, Mademoiselle.

Suzanne You can call me Maria, I can give you the whole afternoon.

Degas Do what I say!

Suzanne Am I doing something wrong, Monsieur Degas?

She remains in the pose.

Puvis used to make me hold the most contorted poses for hours and I didn't complain once in seven years. He even used parts of my body for his boys because I have such good muscles. I got the arm muscles fighting with my mother. He said my arms were streaked with gold. I can be as still as a statue and I don't feel the cold either.

Degas I told you to get dressed.

Suzanne I studied your Pauline's back carefully. Maybe I'm not as young as she is, but backs don't wrinkle from age but from fatigue. That's what I see when I draw them. Your Pauline is tired but I can do tired. I'm tired anyway.

Degas Get dressed and get out now.

Suzanne Monsieur Degas, please tell me what I'm doing wrong.

Degas I asked you here to talk about your new drawings. If you want to be a model, go somewhere else.

Suzanne I learned so much posing for Puvis. And then one day he found one of my drawings. He looked at it for a long time, I think he was impressed but he tore it up and said I was a model not an artist. You say I'm an artist. But I can be both.

Degas No, you can't. An artist is single-minded, obsessed, ruthless. It's an austere life, full of pleasures not taken.

Suzanne I'm all of those things when I model and all of those things when I draw and then I take lots of pleasures during my breaks.

Degas I'll turn away until you are fully clothed.

Suzanne gets dressed, slowly.

Suzanne I have to go back to modelling anyway because I'm broke. My boy is six years old and my mother keeps drinking. I don't mean I would have charged you – not you.

Degas Aren't you living with Toulouse-Lautrec? Doesn't he look after you?

Suzanne We split up.

Degas You left him?

Suzanne He kept saying he wanted to marry me. I know he's a very rich aristocrat and I'm a girl off the streets, but he doesn't care about these things – well, I thought he didn't care, but he has this mother so I decided he needed a little persuading.

Degas And you tried to make him jealous by being unfaithful?

Suzanne (*bursts out laughing*) I was never faithful, it drove him mad. I pretended to commit suicide out of despair for him. I did it really well too. Someone went to get him to see me dying. But just as he was coming ready to propose my stupid drunken mother shouted at the top of her voice that it wouldn't work, he'd see through it. He heard her and ran home and now he won't see me.

I'm very fond of him too, he was the first one to take me seriously. I learned from him.

Degas You won't have learned anything from Lautrec.

Suzanne I didn't have time for Maurice when he was a revolting baby, but now I worry about him. I think my mother gives him wine to keep him quiet.

Degas You can't let trivialities distract you.

Suzanne Money worries aren't trivial.

Degas When I have a line, I hold on to it, I don't let it go. I don't let anything disturb my concentration, especially not money.

Suzanne It's easy for you, you've always had it.

Degas I may have been born into a family of wealthy bankers but my brothers lost it all, speculated – like idiots. Never mind. I endured a public trial. I had to buy back our good name, pay back every penny to the creditors. It took years. I had to move out of a beautiful house, sell everything, even paintings I didn't want to sell. I had no money for myself, but I kept working, working, and I didn't complain. And this is your work. I think I can find some buyers for these drawings, but there should be more. And don't ever think of getting married.

Suzanne Aren't you ever tempted?

Degas I don't want someone looking over my paintings and telling me to make them prettier.

Suzanne But if you fell in love . . .

Degas My dear, I've locked up my heart in a pink ballet shoe.

Degas traces the contour of her arm.

This is beautiful, very beautiful. Don't think I haven't seen that.

But it's for doing work, Suzanne, not modelling.

Don't come back until you have a lot more drawings to show me.

Suzanne about to leave.

But come back soon, come back as soon as you can.

SCENE THREE

'Zoé I'

1893. Zoé discreetly tidies the studio. She spends some time in front a drawing (by Suzanne, perhaps). She arranges the material for soft-ground etching. Looks at other drawings. Continuous movement with some stops in different positions. Something elegant and fluid in the movement and great stillness in the stops, like music. The face remains even.

SCENE FOUR

'Soft Ground Etching'

Degas and Suzanne. Degas shows Suzanne how to make a soft ground etching.

Degas You take a copper plate. I have a few here for us to work on. The plate has to be very smooth, like this. You polish it vigorously until it has a beautiful shine. The more shine, the better the quality of the print later. Now you degrease the plate thoroughly with whitening mixed with a little ammonia.

Suzanne It smells like absinthe. Mmm. Even better.

Degas Pay attention. You rinse the plate and let it dry. Now here is some waxy resin. You dab it on the plate, making a thin layer. This is very even, which is good. The plate must now be handled with great care because any marks will be come out on the print. Now you take this paper and place it very carefully over the soft ground. And then, you draw! Take the pencil.

Suzanne You want me to draw on this?

Degas It's the same as if you were drawing on paper. Go on –

Suzanne What do you want me to draw?

Degas What you want. One of your nudes. This one.

He takes a drawing.

If the pressure is too light it won't reach the soft ground. Let me guide you –

He places her arm gently. a moment from the last scene at this touch. Degas moves away.

I wouldn't dare draw a girl that young and thin and so awkward.

Suzanne Some of your women look awkward.

Degas And they say I hate women. What will they say about you? This girl looks hungry and miserable.

Suzanne She is hungry and she's getting her first period, so she's pretty miserable.

Degas People are afraid of realism, especially the scientific realism I'm after: what a tired back really looks like, what it means to iron all day long – but we have to show these things, in literature as well. Look at Zola.

Suzanne Who?

Degas Emile Zola, Suzanne, a great writer. You'll have to read if you want to be an artist, just as writers need to look at paintings. Zola and I are like twin brothers.
  They say we hate humanity, but we try to show it exactly as it is – bent down, straining for survival, painfully human – as you do by instinct. Those sweating women who iron all day long in their steaming rooms, bent over their work, pressing the iron down in a straight line – releasing it in a curving movement – need to be painted, to be written about. Careful. Don't press so hard –

Suzanne draws. The pencil snaps.

Suzanne Shit. The fucking pencil's broken.
  Sorry about the language. I've ruined it! Fuck! And I've torn the paper.

Degas I distracted you with my talk about Zola.

Suzanne I stopped listening when you started on about ironing.

She tears the paper off the plate and wrinkles it. She looks at the plate.

It's ruined.

Degas We'll start again. This time, you can prepare the plate yourself.

Suzanne No way.

Degas It takes time to learn the technique but etching suits your line and will help you understand drawing in a different way. Let's take another plate and start from the beginning.

Suzanne This is completely bogglingly boring. It's worse than ironing.

Degas If there were no tedium there'd be no enjoyment. We have to do the same thing over and over again.

Suzanne I can't do the same thing again and again.

Degas Repetition makes the good artist. Art does not branch out: it concentrates. They say I repeat myself, but they don't understand I've narrowed my subjects because I'm looking for a truth, layer by layer. It's not pretty or exciting, only real. Now polish that plate.

Suzanne I don't have time.

Degas There's always time when you're learning.

Suzanne Erik gets jealous if I'm away too long.

Degas I thought you were with that Spaniard Utrillo now. He should understand art, he's dabbled in it.

Suzanne Utrillo's gone back to his respectable family in Barcelona, but it doesn't matter because he gave my son his name and that's all I wanted from him.

Degas So who's this one?

Suzanne His name is Erik. Erik Satie. He's a musician and he's teaching me all about music, so you see I'm not that ignorant, and Debussy likes him and you like Debussy so you'd like him, and he's composed pieces for me which I have to say are very slow and solemn – dum-dum-dum – but I'm his first love so I'm teaching him some things too and he's very talented that way and this is what he looks like. I've been waiting to show you.

She presents a small painting.

It looks just like him. You can see he's a bit mad and he's very mystical, although he's taken to sex like a fish to

24

water so I don't know how he's going to square that with the Virgin Mary –

Degas You've done a painting.

Suzanne Isn't it good?

Degas Don't paint.

Suzanne An artist paints.

Degas Painting is not for you.

Suzanne Why? Because it's for men?

Degas No, look at Mary Cassatt. But that's not you.

Suzanne Because she was taught properly? Because she's rich and belongs to your class and she can paint all those little domestic scenes of well-dressed mummies with their fat-cheeked babies and tan doggies? Well, I'm not going to paint doggies.

Degas I haven't painted for two years. I only draw.

Suzanne You painted all your life.

Degas Narratives.

Suzanne Everybody loves your paintings.

Degas And hates these drawings. A narrative carries you along easily. but where's the truth? You might glimpse the truth in the movement of a line, that's all we can hope for. So I give people glimpses, but they have to stand still and pay attention. It's too hard for them so they clamour for a story. Something noisy and emotional. As if there's no emotion in a line, a cross-section of time. It's like that Wagner. The music crashes over you and people feel they've heard something because it's so loud. He calls it total art, but that's typical German bombast. There's no such thing as total art. What you get in Wagner is a lot of scenery and bad Christianity. Where's the truth? Bach, Lully, Rameau, Gluck: they draw.

Suzanne I'll find a way to paint the truth.

Degas Maybe in ten years if you work hard with me, every day.

Suzanne I'm going to do everything I want and I want to paint now. I want to paint a nude.

Degas The nude in painting has always been about an ideal of beauty and it has to be brought to earth with care. If you paint one of your nudes now no one will want to look at it.

Suzanne I'm still going to paint it.

Degas Not if I'm teaching you.

Suzanne I'll teach myself.

Degas You can't teach yourself until you've been taught by a master. Now, please polish that plate.

Suzanne No.

Degas Do what I say.

Suzanne No.

Degas One does not say no to one's teacher.

Suzanne I just want to do something else.

Degas Suzanne, be careful.

Suzanne I don't even know what that means.

Degas I told you to polish the plate.

Suzanne I don't want to.

Degas Then you will leave this studio immediately and never come back. Zoé!

Zoé comes on immediately.

Suzanne Listening again, were you, Zoé? What do you think I'm going to do to your precious Monsieur Degas, hit him over the head with a copper plate?

Zoé You were shouting, that is enough.

Degas Conduct Mademoiselle downstairs, Zoé.

Zoé With pleasure.

Suzanne Happy now? You can have him all to yourself.

Zoé I don't know what you're talking about.

Suzanne You've been waiting for this, haven't you? You don't mind the society ladies or the poor models because they're light, they pass, but someone real, someone with colour in them, you can't stand that. Every time I come here you look me up and down and sigh. I'm too messy for you, is that it?

Zoé We do not like people who are not well brought up, that is all.

Suzanne How the fuck was I supposed to be well brought up? I was illegitimate and raised by a drunken woman who had to leave her village to clean the fleapits of Montmartre. Or did you expect me to learn drawing from Monsieur Degas and politeness from you?

Zoé It wouldn't have done you any harm. I've taught more difficult girls than you.

Suzanne What did you do, run a boot camp?

Degas Zoé was a teacher before she came to me and you will treat her with respect.

Zoé Time for you to leave. Monsieur Degas, your lunch is ready. Please come with me, Mademoiselle.

Suzanne You don't frighten me because I'm not afraid of strong women because I'm one myself and I can see myself out. I won't steal the furniture.

Degas Do not allow Mademoiselle back into my studio.

Zoé I won't. I saw from the beginning that she would never understand discipline.

Suzanne Why should I? I'm going back home and I'll spend the whole afternoon in bed with Erik and then I'll paint him again and he'll compose his weird songs to me and we'll drink a lot and it may not be your kind of art with all its 'discipline', but it's life and it's the art of Montmartre and it's mine and I'm Suzanne and –

Degas Get out.

SCENE FIVE

'Two Women I'

1894. Zoé , Suzanne.

Suzanne I need him. I need him more than anyone.

Zoé I don't want you in his life.

Suzanne You can't stop me from seeing him.

Zoé I can and this time I will.

Suzanne I brought some drawings.

Zoé I told you: he's not here.

Suzanne I need him to look at them. I did a girl bathing from memory. He said that it was as good to draw from memory as from nature but I want to make sure. Please, I've changed.

Zoé We don't believe in quick changes.

Suzanne His work is always changing.

Zoé But he's always the same, the same painter, the same Monsieur Degas with his friends and his habits. Everyone knows who he is and everyone knows me. That's the way we live and we don't need you to disturb us with all your noise.

Suzanne You can't speak for him.

Zoé That's what I do.

Suzanne Who are you, Zoé? You always hide behind that stern mask of yours. Why didn't you stay teaching in the provinces?

Zoé I'm here to look after Monsieur Degas.

Suzanne Women come up from the provinces because they've got into trouble or because they want adventure. Which one was it? You can tell me. Nothing shocks me.
Sometimes I see another face under your face, it's really interesting, it's a woman –

Zoé I don't have time for this.

Suzanne What did you like teaching? You can tell me that much. If you answer, I'll go away. Otherwise we'll stand here for hours like two cats measuring their territory until Monsieur Degas comes back, and you know he can't resist me. Well, he can't resist my drawings.

Zoé Mythology. I liked teaching mythology. Do you know what that is? The gods and goddesses of ancient times.

Suzanne Like you see in the paintings.

Zoé Yes. As you see in the paintings.

Suzanne Gods and goddesses, wow. But Monsieur Degas doesn't do gods and goddesses, he does the real.

Zoé He likes the painters who did. It's not his fault he was born in the wrong century. He likes all those stories where there's some magic. I read him *The Arabian Nights* every day. It's a relief after those newspapers where they're always talking about progress, change and more change, and they forget about all the people left behind.

Suzanne They're the ones I draw. So poverty drove you to Paris?

Zoé My father was a churchwarden.

 Now I have to prepare Monsieur Degas' lunch. So if you don't mind, Mademoiselle –

Suzanne Would you like to see some drawings of mine?

 I think you'll like them. They're mostly of Maurice.

 That's him last year when he was nine. After that he didn't like me to see him in the nude. Although I caught him sleeping, there. What do you think?

Zoé He looks malnourished.

Suzanne He is. My mother drinks all the money I give her and I'm always too busy to notice. He's a very intelligent boy, that's why he keeps getting kicked out of schools. Sometimes I've found him drunk. That's not good at ten, is it?

 That's my mother, the old bat. I've been working, Zoé, I've been working very hard, will you tell Monsieur Degas that? But it's not easy. I'm a mother and I'm frightened for my son. I have to do something, I have to get married.

Zoé Monsieur Degas gave up everything to be an artist, it's not easy for him either.

Suzanne He has the permission of society to be an artist. I'm a woman.

Zoé He never talks about men or women artists but about good and bad ones.

Suzanne You know it's not same. Did you want to be an artist? Is that what happened? It's not even the same for those fur-lined women who paint in opera gloves.

And I may be a bad mother but I'm still devoted to my son, but then I want the time, I want the time to draw in peace. I'm working on a line the way Monsieur Degas showed me and then he gets kicked out of another school and my fingers freeze and I don't know who I am.

They're so fragile at that age, boys. Please, Zoé, help me. You're the only one who can. I want to get better. I miss him so much. I've just seen your other face again. I'll do anything you ask.

Zoé You will have to say you are very sorry to both of us. And then you will never disobey him again.

Suzanne I don't think a talent for obeying –

Zoé It's how you become a good artist.

Suzanne Really? I'll try it then, it'll be a new experience anyway.

Zoé And we don't want to hear any more about marriage.

Suzanne I've got rid of Satie. I'll be good.

Zoé I'll speak to him then.

Suzanne I meant – I'll try.

All right, don't put your mask back on. I'll try very hard to be good. When can I see him?

SCENE SIX

'La Chambre Noire'

1895. Zoé, Degas, Suzanne.
  Suzanne wanders on the periphery.

Degas My new camera. It's the very latest model. With panchromatic plates. The plate is like a mirror, the immaterial image skims the surface. It's a moment. A

31

photographer is like a fisherman, netting the moment. This is my catch of the other night – look, Zoé, these are the pictures I took at the Halévys. Here's a double exposure of the whole family, it's a complete mess, but look at this one. Daniel enlarged it by three.

Zoé It's dear Madame Halévy – but she looks asleep.

Degas I made her pose for so long I think she did fall asleep. I got the hand well, though, see how the light falls on the wrist. Here's Daniel with his mother.

Zoé He looks so serious and refined. I remember him when he was just a studious little boy staring at you and hanging on to every word you said like a hungry dog.

Degas His mother tells me he secretly writes down everything I say. I hope he edits the nonsense.

Zoé And there's Mathilde!

Degas She kept giggling and losing her pose so I had to force her head down on her uncle's shoulders and threaten her if she moved. It took hours. They kept complaining, but we never stopped laughing. Suzanne says I never laugh.

Zoé She hasn't seen you with the Halévys.
  Look, Suzanne, there's Monsieur Halévy, reading as always.

Degas See how the light shimmers on the book. I think I used nine lamps for that one.
  And here's Henriette Taschereau.

Zoé But she's turned into a beauty.
  (*To Suzanne.*) I think Monsieur Degas has a soft spot for her.

Degas Yes. I decided I wanted to marry her, so I approached her father and he said I must go and ask her. So I went to her and told her very politely that her father had given me permission to ask for her hand. And do you know what she did? She held out her hand and gave it to me. I'm almost ready. Suzanne, hand me that lamp. This is my art. Forget all this stuff outside in the *plein air*. Daylight is too easy, I want what is difficult, the atmosphere of lamps, moonlight. Give me the plate. No, not that one!

Suzanne hands him the photographic plate.

Zoé. Stand here. It's stupid to be frightened of photography. It will free art, not ruin it. I walk the streets of Paris, I see something out of the corner of my eye, do I really see it? And then, who am I? In a painting, you always sense the painter looking at the scene. But we're not important. Perhaps this makes us a little anxious because we're no longer there to make sense of things, but nothing makes sense any more anyway. We live in fragments. Zoé, you'll have to stand very still.

Zoé You're not going to photograph me in this old tablier?

Degas Go and change if you want.

Zoé I don't have any nice ones, you've spent all your money acquiring those Delacroix.

Degas I had to have them.

Zoé And I have to have new tabliers. Blue ones. I can't answer the door in a filthy old tablier. What will people think? I won't make you any more tomato and orange jam if you don't buy me some new tabliers.

Degas Then I'll get married and someone else can keep house for me. You'll see, I'll go back to Henriette and explain what it means to ask for a lady's hand.

Zoé You're too old.

Degas How dare you say I'm old when I have all this work to do? Now I'm going to sit down in front of you.

I'll put my chin on my hand to make me look more ferocious. Do I look ferocious? The Halévys say I always look kind but I want to look ferocious. (*To Suzanne.*) Just the way you look right now. How come Suzanne finds it so easy to look ferocious, Zoé? We're almost ready.

Suzanne moves towards the two.

No, Suzanne, we can't have you in the picture. This is my kitchen here – me and the crotchety Zoé. Zoé, look crotchety. Think about your tabliers and the Ingres I'm going to buy next. This is the duration of the instantaneous, the two of us here, always the two of us. Suzanne, you're casting a shadow, move over there and we'll both look at you. No one must move for six minutes. Where are you going? I'm showing you the mysteries of monochrome.

Suzanne I'm not interested in monochrome, I'm interested in bright, vibrant colour. (*She leaves abruptly.*)

Degas Why did she leave? We're having such fun. Go and get her. No! Don't move. Photography requires army discipline. Not one single move for six minutes.

Zoé I thought we were capturing a moment.

Degas We are, it's just a very long one.
   At the end of the six minutes I want you to run out and get Suzanne.

Zoé Where am I going to find her after six minutes?

Degas Don't you know where she lives?

Zoé Of course not.

Degas Suzanne!

Zoé Don't move, you'll ruin the photograph.

Zoé and Degas, frozen.

SCENE SEVEN

'Woman in the Doorway'

1896. Suzanne in an elegant coat, with colour, in the doorway.

Degas Where have you been? You've been missing too many lessons.

Suzanne I've had a lot on my mind.

Degas I wrote to you, but you never answered. I heard you were ill. Are you better? You look a little pale. Do you have any drawings for me?

Suzanne My son's been kicked out of another school. It was my last hope.

Degas However troublesome your son may be you must still work at your cruel and supple drawings. Where are they?

Suzanne So I've decided to go to the country.

Degas You're going on holiday? That's a very good idea. Go somewhere you'll be bored and take a sketchbook with you, but don't stay for more than two weeks because after that the strange becomes familiar.

Suzanne I'm moving to the country.

Degas The country is a place one moves from, Suzanne, not to. Is that not so, Zoé?

Suzanne Paul and I found a school that will take Maurice.
  Paul Mousis is my future husband. He's waiting for me in the carriage. I came to try to explain and to . . . ask for your blessing.

Degas A future husband – in a carriage. My dear, you must still have a fever. Sit down and Zoé will bring you some soup.

Suzanne I'm marrying a very rich banker who's loved me for years, even before Satie, and he's going to buy me a big house and I'll have furniture and things like all your friends in the photographs. I have to hurry because we're shopping for all these clothes and hats and gloves and stockings and umbrellas and parasols and a purse and my wedding dress of course. Next time I come to see you, I'll look like all those puffed-up ladies who visit you and Zoé, you'll have to treat me with respect.

Zoé We treat ladies with politeness, you're the one we treat with respect.

Suzanne It's very complicated being a bourgeois wife, but I learn fast and I'm going to make a very good one. You should have taught me about furniture. I always thought a chair was something you sat on, but I'm learning all about how it decorates and displays good taste.

Degas Good taste is the new disease of the middle classes. Does your banker think you will conceive better children in an apple-green bed? They're now making chamber pots that are so pretty you have to hold your urine back.

Suzanne I want Maurice to be well dressed and healthy and grow up like that Daniel Halévy you and Zoé love so much.

Degas My dear, that is not possible.

Suzanne If I believed anything wasn't possible I wouldn't be here. Maurice will have a serious and respectable father. He can become a banker.

    Pause.

Degas Zoé, will you go downstairs and tell the banker to do his shopping without Suzanne while I show her some drawings? I loved the thickness of your new lines and I've imitated them in my drawings. And there's some work I want you to do on your women bathing.

Suzanne Monsieur Degas, I really am getting married.

Degas Zoé told me you promised not to.

Suzanne I've changed.

Degas You can change again. Zoé, what are you waiting for? Tell Monsieur the Banker he's made a mistake.

Suzanne That's what his mother says, but Paul says bankers never make mistakes and if they do, it's their job to cover them up. He'll never change his mind about me. Monsieur Degas, please understand. I need this and I'm going to marry him.

Degas This is a moment of discouragement. We all have them, but you have to work through these moments. The best is to go back to the beginning, start again with something very simple.

Suzanne Paul will build me a big studio in the country and I'll paint very large canvases with a lot of colour.

Degas I haven't given you permission to paint large canvases.
  I might allow you to try a few small ones under my guidance. We'll go to the Louvre together and find something for you to copy.

Suzanne I have to do what I want.

Degas No. You do not have to do what you want. You made one decision in your life, to be an artist. Is that not so, Zoé? Did I not hear correctly?

Zoé You heard correctly.

Degas Then you do not do what you want but what you must.

Suzanne I feel I must paint.

Degas You do not decide that. You have a master to teach you. I am that master.

You did not go to an art school. I have worked at making that up for you. And now I decide what is good for you and I have decided that it is not good for you to leave Paris.

Zoé, why are you still here? Go tell Monsieur Mousis to move to the country without her. Tell him Monsieur Degas said so. Now let's catch up on lost time.

Suzanne My son is in that carriage.

Degas The banker can teach him mathematics.

Suzanne He won't if I'm not his wife.

Degas You're too protective of that son of yours anyway. He'll behave better if you stop fussing over him.

Suzanne You don't understand.

Degas I understand painting, literature, music and France. What else is there to understand?

Suzanne There's love.

Zoé Monsieur Degas understands love better than you. He understands its pain, its sacrifice, he understands devotion, things you don't even suspect. He's older than you and you ought to listen to what he says.

Suzanne I will never forget what you taught me, Maître, but I am ready to do it on my own now.

Degas You're like a child who thinks he can flap his wings and fly. An artist doesn't appear out of nowhere. There is a history, a country, a tradition. An artist works the way a horse ploughs a field, not looking to left or right, obeying the tradition, and fitting into it the way the horse fits into the groove and then moves forward, breaking up new ground. I am born after Ingres and Delacroix, I take up where they left off, just as another horse will replace me. I am teaching you to be that horse, to take the yoke, to work. Sometimes the accolades will come, sometimes they won't but you must know who you are and what your duty is. Can you not understand what you owe to the tradition?

Suzanne You left it.

Degas I left the way a son might leave his father's house, but he continues the family values and he respects his inheritance.

Suzanne I never had a father. I don't have an inheritance. I made my own way. I learned by myself and I'm going to do it differently. And I'm going to make great big canvases full of colour, and maybe they won't be Degas but they'll be Valadons. They'll be new and shocking and me! And the twentieth century is coming and we'll sweep tradition out the door like the dust it is.

Degas I taught you, I nourished you, I even loved you. You insult me, you betray art, you threaten France!

Suzanne I'm sorry about what I said – you know what I'm like, I don't want to argue, I came to get your blessing, please, Maître.

Degas My curse! You won't paint. Ducks and geese are not conducive to good art. Even the *plein air* painters only venture out for an afternoon before running back to Paris. The bourgeoisie exists to dull the sharp edges of the soul. I'm the one saw your spirit, your talent. I treated it like the precious thing it is, and now you crumple it and throw it back in my face like a bad sketch. Go then, wallow in the torpor of your new-found comfort.

Suzanne Maître: look at me, look at what I am. Try to understand what it is like to live in fear, not of poverty – I don't care about that – but of disappearing altogether. My son is thirteen, disturbed, killing himself with drink and disappearing in front of me. And if he does kill himself? What will I be then? You have safety all around you, with your education, Zoé, with your friends. I have no one, nothing but what I have taken myself by force – and it can all disappear. Why do you hate me for wanting what was given to you at birth? What's wrong with a little furniture if it gives me some substance? You're Monsieur Degas, why can't I be Madame and have people take their hats off, noticed, there, solid. Can't you understand how difficult it is for me because I'm never sure I'm there? Even you, you're interested in my drawings but drawings are easily erased and you only want to hear about my life when I can entertain you with something amusing.

Degas When I draw my dancers, I can guess at their sordid lives, the lovers, the drunken mothers, but that is background, what we see is the line of their arabesque. We are dancers, Suzanne, trying for those beautiful arabesques. The rest is detail.

Suzanne My life is not a fucking detail.

And if it is to you, then my going away is also a detail and you won't mind it so much.

Degas Why ascribe so much importance to life, Suzanne? Art is important. Stay with me and I'll prove it to you.

Stay.

Pause.

Suzanne I can't.

Degas moves to touch her.

Degas You are deceiving yourself.

Suzanne I have to go.

Degas You ought to have more pride. This is a waste.

Suzanne I promise that no hour I have spent with you has ever been wasted. Goodbye, Maître.

Degas turns away.

Zoé?
  He'll forgive me, won't he, Zoé? He always does.

Zoé I won't.

Suzanne Because I want to live?

Zoé Because you want to cheat.

Suzanne leaves. Degas sits in dejection. Zoé takes up Le Figaro. *Monochrome.*

SCENE EIGHT

'Second Photograph: Zoé Reading the Newspaper'

25 November 1897. Zoé reading the newspaper. Degas and Zoé. Zoé reads from Le Figaro.

Zoé Here's an article by Emile Zola.

Degas About painting? Does he mention me?

Zoé It's about that young captain who was accused of spying for the Germans. You were interested in the case at the time.

Degas Dreyfus! He was passing secrets about French artillery. Has he escaped from prison? Why is Zola bringing it up? Read.

Zoé 'A military tribunal has condemned of treason a man who may be innocent.'

Degas Read that again.

Zoé 'A military tribunal has condemned of treason a man who may be innocent.'

Degas There's a contradiction in that sentence.

Zoé Why a contradiction if the man is innocent?

Degas The French military tribunal found him guilty of treason, therefore he is guilty of treason, Q.E.D. Where's Zola's logic? But then he told me he never got his baccalaureate. It shows.

Zoé I still don't follow.

Degas Dreyfus is guilty by the authority of the French military and Zola ought to respect that. We're not talking about mines or painters here but about military security and the honour of France. Read on.

Zoé 'It is very simple and very clear if you take the affair for what it is: a miscarriage of justice, most deplorable but nonetheless possible. Lawyers can make mistakes, so too can the military.'

Degas No! The military can never make a mistake.

Zoé Isn't it run by men?

Degas The military is an entity protecting the honour of France, therefore it cannot make a mistake.
   What can Zola possibly say to prove the contrary?

Zoé 'Lies multiply, serious newspapers repeat the stupidest stories, the whole nation seems prey to insanity . . .'

Degas You see? Question the honour of the French military and the reputation of the French nation comes tumbling down like a badly constructed house.
   'The nation seems prey to insanity –' It's Zola who's gone insane, his books have had bad reviews.

Zoé 'And if political expedience should delay the course of justice, it would compound the original mistake, which would only defer the eventual outcome and aggravate it even more.'

Degas That's Zola for you, his sentences are so complicated you lose the argument. What is he saying?

Zoé I think Zola is saying Captain Dreyfus is innocent. What if he is innocent, Monsieur Degas?

Degas Why does no one understand that he can't be because he was found guilty? But even if he were innocent he should accept that he's guilty because of the authority and honour of the French military. If you can die for your country why can't you be dishonoured for your country? France comes first to a Frenchman. But Captain Dreyfus is not interested in the honour of France or of the army. He's interested in himself. And he's being defended by Jews who think he is being accused because he is a Jew. They believe one Jewish individual is more important than the interests of the French nation. But if you're in France, you have to be French first. We can't all go around saying we have different bits of ancestry, Italian or Jewish, and that gives us a right to question everything. We are French. The Jews don't understand patriotism.

Zoé Monsieur Degas, that's a large generalisation.

Degas Generalisations are how you form opinions. And you must agree with me, Zoé.

Zoé I think you ought to discuss all of this with the Halévys.

Degas I will never see the Halévys again.

Zoé But they're your closest friends!

Degas They're Jewish.

Zoé But they always were and you've loved them all. Daniel is like a son to you.

Degas The last time I was there they were talking about the two people I hate the most, Dreyfus and Wagner. Imagine liking the music of that awful German. It's unpatriotic. We must protect France from Wagner and Dreyfus.

Zoé You dine there three times a week. You're expected tonight.

Degas I wrote to them this morning. I will never set foot in their house again.

Zoé Where will you go now?
   What do I tell Daniel if he comes here?

Degas Oh, if he comes . . .
   You see the damage Dreyfus has done?
   Pissarro crosses the street when he sees me.

Zoé Mary Cassatt doesn't come any more.

Degas I told her to stop painting baby Jesus with his English nanny.

   Pause.

I have a social conscience, Zoé. I believe in the voice of the French peasant, I was angered by the repression of the people during the Commune –

   Pause.

– but I served in the artillery, I defended France against the Prussians, it cost me my health and my eyesight, but I did it gladly as a Frenchman – I obeyed authority like all Frenchman throughout history. Zola never fought for France. He doesn't understand obedience, how the individual must fold himself up in order to fit into this greater entity, the greatest nation on earth.

44

Zoé But justice?

Degas The clamour of the individualist.

Pause.

It's quiet here, isn't it?
  The evenings are long . . .
  Have you heard anything of Suzanne?

Pause.

Read me the rest of the article.

Zoé There is only one line.

Degas Read it.

Zoé You won't like it.

Degas Idiocy doesn't fill me with anger but with pity.

Zoé 'The truth is marching forward and nothing will
stop it.'

Degas The truth! What does he know about the truth?
he's a writer!

Zoé I'm still concerned about justice.

Degas Justice? What is justice? Was there any justice
for my brothers when they were misled by unscrupulous
speculators? Didn't you tell me the Prussians invaded
your village? Was it just that we were defeated and I gave
up my eyesight for nothing? Justice is a heavenly dream,
but we are on earth and we are in France.

He looks at a drawing of Suzanne.

The truth is simple. My country. The shape of an arm.
  A line. No more.

'Death Mask'

1901. Degas is sculpting a small figure of a ballet dancer in clay.

Degas I am doing everything a man does when he wants to die alone, without any happiness whatsoever. When I am invited to dinner I complain loudly about any subject people bring up. I rail against the Jews when my best friends are Jews. I hate the Protestants for good measure. The Louvre wants a painting from me: I refuse the honour. A friend sells a painting of mine, I return one of his in the post. Mind you, I was right to do that, I gave the painting as a gift, not as an asset. My paintings sell for high prices, I insult the buyers. No one wants to see me any more and I want to see no one. Young painters come to adore me, I make fun of them. I chased Suzanne away . . . I used to have wit, it is gone. Old age is nothing more than the loss of joy. How did I lose my joy? How did it become arthritic? I followed a path with certainty. I didn't know it would get dark. I worked, life ebbed away. And now I can't even pee properly.

And yet, I still work. I work. It is not about what one is doing but about what one might do one day.

I open my eyes wide to the light but there is almost none there. So I feel with my hand the line of a hip or the insertion of a muscle which I will model in wax.

Horses. Ballerinas. This one. I call it 'Dancer with a Tambourine'. Her body works, every muscle shaped for its leaps and stretches. But look at her face. The skin is pulled tight in pain. No life. No joy. No expression. Almost no face. There was a model for the body but I did not use her face. The face is myself. When they ask you about this sculpture, tell them this is the death mask of Edgar Degas.

'*The Bourgeoise*'

1904. Suzanne, very well dressed in a kind of sombre but opulent elegance. Gloves, hat, etc. Degas is more dishevelled.
Suzanne has a large carton.

Degas Madame.

He bows with some irony.

On a shopping trip from the country? You're taking in the sights?

Suzanne looks at some pastels.

Suzanne That's beautiful.

Degas Same old thing. Bodies and hair, lots of hair. For you hair was natural, I've worked hours, days, months, years on women's hair. Men don't have hair – they do, but it doesn't move. But you must only be interested in the hats that go over the hair. You've come to Paris to see your milliner?

Suzanne Please don't be angry with me.

Degas A little card from you every year in your saw-like handwriting. I answer, 'Please let the writer of this note come with a box under her arm. A box full of those wicked drawings for her old friend.' No reply. Years pass. Not one visit. Not one drawing. I work hard for you, people are buying your drawings, but you don't care. Although there is a large box under her arm. Perhaps I am mistaken. Perhaps she has brought me something. I'll wait.

Suzanne You haven't changed.

47

Degas I'm older and more blind and no one likes me. They won't forgive me for not supporting Dreyfus. Did you?

Suzanne Who?

Degas Even in the thick silences of the provincial mind, they must have talked about Dreyfus at your dinners?

Suzanne I never listen to anything at those dinners.

Degas It seems he was innocent. Zola was right, but he was murdered for it. Where was I? One must work. That box is pleasingly large.
   May I look?

Suzanne You would approve of my son, he works all the time. I'm very proud of him.

Degas Children and furniture give the bourgeoise a sense of history.

Suzanne He drank even more in the country – he started exposing himself to pregnant women and we had to put him in an asylum.

Degas Zola would attribute all that to heredity. Didn't you once tell me his father wasn't Utrillo but a drunken clown you slept with one night?

Suzanne I don't care who his father was, I'm his mother.

Degas It seems they blocked the chimney of the hovel Zola lived in. It was like one of his novels. May I just lift the cover of the box? Have a peep?

Suzanne When Maurice was in the asylum I taught him to draw.
   He took to it and spent more hours drawing than I ever did. He is obsessed – like you. He made painting after painting.

Degas Good for him. But what have you done during these long and dark years?

Suzanne I had a house to run, I made a beautiful garden, I even made some furniture.

Please, you've always been my friend, look at these paintings.

Degas These are not yours?

Suzanne They're Maurice's. His paintings are even beginning to sell, mostly to Americans.

Degas Americans turn everything they touch into a commodity. I sell to them too, but I don't boast about it.

Suzanne takes out the paintings, they are all very small.

Suzanne Remember when you refused to look at my drawings, Maître? Look.

Degas looks.

Degas Montmartre. Of course they'll sell.

Suzanne I told you they were good.

Degas I said they would sell, not that they were good. Surely you can see.

Suzanne I see great talent and such facility.

Degas Talent perhaps, facility yes, but look, there is no movement. Nothing in these paintings moves. These are not paintings, they are postcards. Now Madame, although I have time for artists, I have little patience with women of the world who drag their sons behind them like performing poodles. So you must excuse me –

He seizes one of her drawings.

I went to Zola's funeral but I missed the funeral of Suzanne Valadon. Look at her, Madame. She was so lean and supple. Strong too. So seductive. So real.

Zoé will see you out, Madame Mousis, don't bother to come back.

49

But that artist I used to know, that Suzanne Valadon, if I'm mistaken and she's not dead, tell her she is always welcome here.

Suzanne We are one and the same.

Degas No, Madame, not the same.

He picks up a glove Suzanne has dropped.

These are very fine.

He puts them gently in Suzanne's hand and holds that hand for a moment.

And the hand is still beautiful.

He puts the glove on Suzanne's hand. Buttons it.

The glove is perfectly tight.
Where's the movement now?

SCENE ELEVEN

'Zoé II'

Zoé, alone, in black.

Zoé There will be one or two photographs of me. One or two lines in biographies. My name: Zoé Clozier. Born 1840. I will die in 1919, two years after Degas.

I know more about him than anyone, but I'm not asked. And I wouldn't say anything anyway. But there isn't a detail I'm not aware of.

We are more intimate than a couple, much more. Sometimes he threatens to marry to put my nose out of joint. But he won't. I could tell you – but I won't.

There were adventures when he was young, but he won't marry. No. There's not much there now – well, I've seen him naked.

In the photograph, I look hard. If I'd been painted you might see devotion. But what is that? When they show religious devotion it's always a face upturned. It's not really like that. It's like a line. There is always a line, from him to me. Every movement of his leads to mine. It's the other way, too. Because, you see, I work as hard as he does. I don't mean cooking, cleaning, shopping, I do that too. No: I work like an artist, attentive, obsessive. He is my work. I don't mean I create him. But I watch him. I see him clearly. I know him in his every movement. That's my work. Isn't that what he does?

SCENE TWELVE

'Two Women II'

Suzanne comes on with a folder under her arm. She is radiant, loose, colourful, bohemian. The women embrace.

Suzanne You haven't changed. You're eternal.
Where is he? I have so much to tell him.

Zoé He's been ill. Please don't tell him I wrote to you or he'll refuse to see you.

Suzanne I came as soon as I had your letter.

Zoé I've never asked anyone for anything.

Suzanne What is it, Zoé?

Zoé I'm asking you now: help me.

Suzanne Zoé!

Zoé We have to move. We've been here twenty years but the building is going to be torn down. I can't tell him any of that. I'm getting old. You'll have to tell him.

Suzanne But I haven't seen him in seven years.

Zoé How could you neglect us like that?

Suzanne I'm sorry – life. I'm preparing a solo exhibition and then Maurice is still a virgin at twenty-eight and I'm trying to do something about that.

Zoé He's crumbling in my hands. He was never good at being young, but he's hopeless at being old. Whenever I say something about moving he makes me read another of the thousand and one tales from *The Arabian Nights*. My eyes are going. You'll tell him he has to move whether he likes it or not.

Suzanne I'm his pupil, I can't say that.

Zoé You'll find a way. He always melts when he sees you.

Suzanne I'm not the same as I was.

Zoé He's coming – he must have heard your voice. I'm counting on you. Did you bring some drawings? How many? Are they good?

Suzanne I think so . . .

Zoé They have to be your best.

SCENE THIRTEEN

'The Male Nude'

Degas, Suzanne, Zoé in and out.

Degas Madame? You've come to visit an old invalid?

He kisses her hand.

I smell work.

Suzanne I divorced him. The court decided he had been the perfect husband so I've lost everything. We're back in Montmartre. I'm poor, I'm happy, I'm working and –

Degas You've come back to your teacher?

Suzanne I'm in love.

Degas Not another marriage, Suzanne!

Suzanne Here he is: André Utter. My lover.

She takes out many drawings of a male nude. Degas whistles.

Degas How naughty you are.
You are the first woman to draw a male nude.
Even I don't do it any more.

Suzanne Isn't he beautiful?

Degas You're kinder to him than to your female nudes.
You've idealised him.

Suzanne He really does look like that.

Degas But you've made him look twenty-five.

Suzanne He is twenty-five. He's younger than Maurice.

Degas What a scandal you are. And this is Maurice? This line is good, you've caught the mechanism of a gesture.

Suzanne André befriended Maurice and they became very close. That's how I met him. Now Maurice is so jealous he's taken to calling me Joan of Arc and prostrating himself before me, so we have put him back in an asylum. But he's painting and André is selling the paintings. He sells Maurice's story with it – you know, tormented artist from Montmartre, that goes down well and we're a success.

Degas In my day artists were never 'successes' and certainly not on the strength of their biography.

Suzanne It's the new century, Maître. We tear down, we rebuild. I'm exhibiting in the Gallery of the Twentieth

Century with a painter called Picasso. André knows him and the other new painters and we spend our nights talking about art. And when I tell these artists I know you, they become very shy. They worship you.

Degas You worship the dead.

I'm making sculptures now, ballerinas. I would have liked to paint the grand classical scenes, but history only allows me to paint women in tubs. One has to take one's place in history. The age of the epic is over, this is the age of the keyhole.

Suzanne I'm painting landscapes.

Degas I'm doing landscapes with figures in them. We are made to look at each other, Suzanne. Our responsibility is to show, in detail, a few people with their aspirations and their frailties. If we don't look at human beings, at their bodies, where will pity and tenderness come from? Isn't that what the world needs? Who will love human beings if we stop painting them?

Suzanne Picasso says he can't imitate your line so he shows women from the back and the front at once, but I remember all the stuff you said about power in simplicity so I'm working on that.

Degas You haven't forgotten your old master, then?

Suzanne Forget you? Your words are always ringing in my ears: work, work, work.

Degas Then you've come back to yourself. And you've come back to me. We must celebrate! Zoé can bring us some of her orange and tomato jam, but we've lost so much time. I'll show you how to use tracing paper with pastels, it's a way to play with colour and I know you love colour.

Suzanne I want to make a painting from these drawings.

Degas Yes, that too. But these drawings will take charcoal and pastel very well, it will be a good transition. Shall we start?

Zoé comes in.

Suzanne Yes, Maître, please.

Zoé Suzanne has something to tell you. Don't you, Suzanne.

Suzanne Do I? I love these –

Degas Those are my Russian dancers.

Suzanne They look wild.

Zoé You do have something to tell Monsieur Degas.

Degas Zoé, we have so much work to do – go away.

Zoé doesn't move.

Zoé Suzanne.

Suzanne Zoé and I were talking . . .

Degas And when women get together it's not to talk about art – but never mind, I'm so happy today. Here, here's the tracing paper –

Zoé Monsieur –

Suzanne Monsieur Degas.

Degas The answer is no. Now, let's get to work.

Suzanne They will demolish the building.

Degas They can demolish me with the building. I have twenty-six of your drawings here and drawings by Ingres and Delacroix, and a new Gauguin, and I'm not moving anything.

Zoé Suzanne will help you with your new studio.

Suzanne Yes, marriage is a very good lesson in decorating.

Degas I'm not moving.

Suzanne You have to.

Degas I don't have to do anything.

Suzanne But you told me how often you moved when you were young.

Degas I'm an old tree now and my roots go deep. A tree? What a pretty *plein air* picture that is. Dust, that's what you called me once. French dust. Brushed aside for the violence and the rigid lines of the new century. And the Prussians are rattling their sabres again – do they think I can't hear them? It's that Wagner. No, there's someone called Schoenberg now, doesn't even bother with notes any more. Well, I'm not making way for any demolition squad, whether it's Wagner or Schoenberg or a Parisian landlord. Never!

Zoé It's time for your rest.

Degas No rest ever, only wormwood time eating Degas away, boring holes through his life, munch munch, but Degas makes a last stand. Degas stays here. I'll chain myself to the floor.

He goes down on his knees.

Every inch of this studio has layers of hours worked, battles with the infirmity of being human, discoveries, false starts, triumphs. I've paced this floor for twenty years, I can recount every painting I did from my footsteps. Can't you see the colours? Don't let them move the old bear from his cave, Suzanne, don't let them move me from myself, pity.

Suzanne Maître . . .

He stops himself.

Degas The male nude doesn't look like your beautiful new lover. Women sag on the outside, we sag inside – we don't notice and suddenly the spirit's fallen. Look carefully, Suzanne. Here's your male nude.

SCENE FOURTEEN

'The Flâneur'

Degas Six, Boulevard de Clichy: here lives the man of sorrow. Leave quickly. Rue des Martyres: time here, years ago, the dance master and his ballerinas, up there. Go back to my studio, thirty-seven, Rue Victor Massé. Gone! Come here every day, watch my life turn to rubble. Keep walking. The Music Hall still stands, lights too bright. Where am I going? Rue Douai, twenty-two, the Halévys. Daniel comes down and walks with me sometimes, doesn't hold a grudge, sweet boy. So many good hours. Ludovic's beautiful face when he lay dead. Open the curtains. Light. Friends. No more friends. Walk on. Twenty-one, Rue de Bruxelles. Zola asphyxiated, no one confessed. Told him there was no justice. Empty now. Where am I? Place Pigalle. I never take models from the Place Pigalle. Number nine, La Nouvelle Athènes. Meet, talk. Zola, Manet, dead, that Irishman George Moore, wanted to write about me, what was there to say? Painted 'L'Absinthe' on the terrace. Who posed? Two actors? Got her hair right. Keep walking. Where am I going? Climb, climb up the hill, turn, climb. Moulin de la Galette. Stopped turning last year. Must be the only one who didn't paint it. Too rectangular. Keep climbing. Different air up here. Montmartre. Where am I? Place du Tertre, new generation sets up its easels, hope splashes on the stones. Can't breathe. Where am I going to piss? Lots of alleyways, quick. Where am I going? Rue Cortot, twelve, Rue Cortot. Suzanne!

'The Artist's Studio'

1914. Suzanne's studio. Degas. Suzanne.

Degas You never come to me any more. I come to you.

Suzanne We have so many shows to prepare.

Degas You're famous.

Suzanne Maurice is famous, but we have to keep him from trading his paintings for alcohol. He can't keep up with the demand from the Americans.

Degas The Americans are hovering over us like vultures over a corpse. Is it my eyes or is darkness descending over Europe?

Suzanne André says Germany will declare war any minute now. He wants to volunteer.

Degas The male nude? Still beautiful?

Suzanne He drinks, he womanises, I shout, I work. He looks after our affairs, we seem to be rich.

Degas Soon there will ne no art, only commerce.

Suzanne I'm glad not to be poor any more, it makes me more free.

Degas We are never free, only held in the tight fist of one god or another. We worship ours because he holds the lightning that makes us see the truth. Only a flash, a moment, a detail, a line. Show me a drawing, my dear.

Suzanne I'm only painting.

Pause.

Look at them, just this once, look at this one. You know you can see when you want to. Please, Maître, I'll never ask you again.

Pause. Suzanne places a painting: Degas. A long moment.

Degas There is no history here.

Suzanne It's a portrait.

Degas When I paint there is all the history of painting behind what I do. You do not have that education.

Suzanne This is the twentieth century. I don't need education.

Degas You have to stand inside history.

Suzanne I only want to know if you think my painting is good or not.

Degas I can't separate myself from history, the hierarchy of excellence.

Suzanne I never went for hierarchies.

Degas Women understand almost everything but not hierarchy.

Suzanne Please don't tell me you don't think women can paint, not after what you've done for me.

Degas You can paint, Suzanne, but you don't integrate yourself into the line of history. Because of that, you risk being forgotten. You see, no one will know how to judge your work.

Suzanne I don't care.

Degas You are French. We are obsessed with our reputation. That's what makes us French.

Suzanne Most of the young painters aren't even French.

Degas My family came from Italy and New Orleans. That didn't prevent me from being French.

Suzanne I'm looking for the truth, not for national identity. She's not a statement, she's a real woman, solid, not beautiful because I can never flatter my subjects.

Degas The history of painting tells us that women are beautiful.

Suzanne Well, history got it wrong and can go fuck itself.

Degas How dare you speak like that to me!

Suzanne Forgive me, everybody swears in the modern world. Maître, you told me once how hurt you were that your father didn't like your work. And then one day he saw a painting up in the corner of an exhibit which he loved but he couldn't read the name. He asked if you knew who'd done it. It was by you. What would you say if you saw my painting up there in a corner and didn't know it was by me?

Degas You've left me behind, that's what I would say: you've left me behind.

SCENE SIXTEEN

'Self-Portrait'

Suzanne Where does the beauty of a face go? It inverts, hardens, sucked in, sucked down. Eyes and mouth sag with the force of gravity – 'gravitas'. The downward spiral of experience. The skin thickens – well, it has to, when you're exposed to criticism, jealousy, mockery.

I remember when Renoir painted me, all soft curves, shimmering face, minute hands. What's left of that red-haired fifteen-year-old full of grace? Does strength wipe out beauty in a woman?

Hard face. The face that allows the young lover to be unfaithful. The shit! And he thinks I don't smell the whores on him? The face of the cuckolded woman. Laughable.

Observe the thickness of the neck. This woman drank a lot, fucked a lot, played and worked hard, lived.

The face of success. They call me the best woman painter of this century. They wouldn't say 'best painter', would they, they always have to put 'woman' in there. Not much female in this face, so, a necklace, in homage to the woman.

Sagging breasts. Is that what he looks for? Young women whose breasts are soft, smooth, round, upright? Face of unrequited desire. I pull him towards me, I see the spasm of reluctance, the moment of hesitation, and I see other women in that little gap of fatigue, that's when I scream and scratch and hit him.

The ageing woman. No, the ageing painter. I'm at the height of my powers, so why am I sad if my face is in decline? Tenderness, Degas would say. His self-portraits were always full of tenderness. But tenderness belongs to the last century. The war has ripped it out of us. I'm modern. I don't like humanity.

He started it all, the uncompromising line, the tired female body, but he never showed the face. Couldn't face the tired face.

Worries thicken, hunch the shoulders. Maurice, his rage, his insanity, and now, worst of all, religion. Can you believe it?

Not a face to be looked at. This is a face that sees.

She paints her signature.

'Suzanne Valadon. Self-Portrait.'

1917.

And my poor master is ill.

SCENE SEVENTEEN

'Chiaroscuro'

1917. Degas slumped on a chair in an old dressing gown. Zoé, Suzanne.

Zoé He was always lost here. He won't recognise you.

Suzanne I think he will.

Zoé His niece is here now. She's taken over the flat. She's trying to take him over as well and he's too weak to defend himself. She treats me like a maid. As if I haven't looked after him half of his life, as if I don't know him better than anyone. I think she's trying to poison him, so she can sell his work. She's out now, but if she comes back she'll tell you to leave. She doesn't want him to see anyone. Not that many people come.

Suzanne He's still much loved.

Zoé He was always alone, really. Some men like their misery.

Suzanne He follows his own rules, that's all.

Zoé He never wanted to hurt anyone except with that Jewish business. Men have too many opinions, in my view, it's bad for their health. He won't know who you are.

Suzanne He's always known who I am.

Zoé I'll try to keep the niece downstairs but I don't know if I can.

Suzanne Zoé! Are you frightened?

Zoé He was my strength. I can't see without him.

Degas stirs. Zoé leaves.

Suzanne Maître . . . It's me, Suzanne . . .

Degas doesn't respond.

Your terrible Maria . . . Remember when you used to call me by my model's name to tease me?

Degas Maria . . . Maria Cassatt?

Suzanne Not that rich American flower-painting bitch – how dare you think of her!

Degas (*faint smile*) You must be Suzanne, Suzanne Valadon. Are you still drawing, excellent artist? You moved me here and then you abandoned me.

Suzanne André was wounded at the front and I had to look after him. Then he went back to his drink and his floozies. I'm alone.

Degas Good, you can work.

Suzanne I hate being alone. Maurice wants to marry a religious bigot.

Degas I know about bigotry. The shadow that glides under the doorway and then blows out all the lamps, one by one. I took a position, it was expected. Why should artists think better than anyone else? All those passionate opinions, for what? But they never seeped into my work. Keep looking, sacrifice everything, and in the end, accept oblivion.

Suzanne Not you. Everyone tells stories about you, you're quoted all over Paris. But I never say anything about you now because I don't know how to describe you truthfully. I don't even know how to say what you've done for me. My lifeline.

Pause.

I'm not good at being grateful. I neglect you and you always forgive. A true master. And when you looked at

something I did, it lit up for me. I hate words, Monsieur Degas, I only want to say – thank you.
My teacher. Master.

She bends down to kiss his hand. Degas starts. He suddenly grabs her hand and holds it up to the light.

Degas Look at that arm.
Why didn't I draw that arm?

Suzanne I offered to model for you, you refused.

Degas I had to.

He turns her arm in the light.

You were so beautiful sitting in that chair, the towel draped around you, the light on the curve of your back.

Suzanne I would have done anything for you.

Degas I stood there. I knew I mustn't move forward. Not a step. It wasn't easy.

Suzanne I would have been your mistress if you asked.

Degas I knew that. It's not that I didn't want . . . I could draw your back now.
You were my pupil.

Suzanne I would have been both. I loved you.

Degas Both? Do you think so?
There's a drawing of yours over there, bring it to me.

Suzanne does so.

I can still see your wicked lines. I loved those. You.
We could have both? I don't think so . . . you wouldn't have respected . . . Both? . . . We'll never know.

He caresses her arm.

I could have drawn this arm. Caressed this skin with colour. I'm ending my life without ever having tasted happiness.

Suzanne My austere master.

Degas I did taste beauty and I made beauty.

He caresses her hair.

Your magnificent hair.
  Work, my love, work hard.

He traces the shape of her arm.

Remember the line.

He goes still.
  Suzanne.
  Zoé comes back on.

Fade.